بسم الله الرحمن الرحيم

"The house of al-Arqam is the house of Islām"

Al-Ḥākim (d. 405/1014) in *al-Mustadrak ʿala al-Ṣaḥiḥayn* (6185)

Ibn ʿAqīl al-Ḥanbalī's Essay on

Islamic Manners

فصول الآداب ومكارم الأخلاق المشروعة

تأليف

الإمام العلامة أبي الوفاء علي بن عقيل بن محمد
ابن عقيل بن عبد الله البغدادي الظفري
المتوفى سنة ٥١٣ هـ

Abu-l-Wafā' ʿAlī b. ʿAqīl al-Ḥanbalī (d. 513/1119)

Translated with an Introduction & Notes by Jewel Jalil

DAR AL-ARQAM

ISBN: 978 1 8384897 2 4

British Library Cataloguing in Publishing Data
A catalogue record for this book is available from the British Library

First edition, 2021

Prepared and published by Dar al-Arqam Publishing
Birmingham, United Kingdom

www.daralarqam.bigcartel.com
Email: daralarqam@hotmail.co.uk

Translated by Jewel Jalil

Printed in Turkey by Mega | export@mega.com.tr

Ibn ʿAqīl al-Ḥanbalī's Essay on

ISLAMIC MANNERS

Abu-l-Wafāʾ ʿAlī b. ʿAqīl al-Ḥanbalī (d. 513/1119)

Translated with an Introduction & Notes by Jewel Jalil

DAR AL-ARQAM

Contents

Acknowledgements

In the winter of 2016, I started teaching Ibn 'Aqīl's *Fuṣūl al-ādāb* to a small group of students in London. During the next few months (between January and April), on a weekly basis, I translated small sections of the Arabic text for our lessons until we finished the entire essay. It was a wonderful few months. This English translation was originally published as an addendum to *An Epitome of Ḥanbalī Substantive Law* (2018) but owing to the essay's importance, it is being published again separately. This new bilingual edition, with its parallel Arabic text, will allow readers to access the original Arabic and hopefully assist with vocabulary building, oracy, and future translations. In the new edition, I also included a short introduction to prepare the readers. It is hoped the translation will be received well owing to its style and simplicity.

I thank Allāh for letting me complete the translation, and moreover permitting me to teach such a wonderful treatise. I would like to thank my friend Parvez Ahmed for gifting me a copy of the Arabic text. I am very grateful to my few students for enduring with me on this long journey, and being patient with me when I cancel or have prolonged gaps between our lessons. I appreciate the West Euston Partnership's team for allowing us to use their venue to hold these lessons. I would like to express my gratitude to my family and friends for their love and support. My wife, Shireen, and my children, Yahya, Safiyya, Zakariya, Abdullah and Abdurrahman – for everything you endure, I appreciate you all very much. My father, Abdul Jalil, and my late mother, Kulsum Jalil, may Allāh reward you both abundantly. Last but not least, I must extend my appreciation to the editorial team at Dar al-Arqam Publications for their patience and support.

Jewel Jalil
London, February 2021

Translator's Introduction

Translation as a process

Translation is a process of changing the original written text (the source text or ST) in the original verbal language (the source language or SL) into a written text (the target text or TT) in a different verbal language (the target language or TL). In short, it is rendering the meaning of a text into another language in the way the author intended the text.[1] Therefore, it is incumbent to fully comprehend the ST for the correct application of the TL syntax and lexis. Inadequate understanding of the ST brings about errors pertaining to syntax and grammar in the TL. Thus, thorough research is required to fully understand the ST and become acquainted with the subject matter. According to Nida, the 'basic requirements' of a translation must consist of four elements. Firstly, it must make sense. Secondly, it must convey the spirit and manner of the original. Thirdly, it must have a natural and easy form of expression. Fourthly, it must produce a similar response.[2]

Methodology and issues associated with the translation

Ibn 'Aqīl's *Fuṣūl al-ādāb* is a short essay on Islamic manners. The objective of this translation is to render the essay into English which will be clear and concise. The language employed in the translation has been kept simple and modern. The translation was based on the Arabic edition of Dr. 'Abdullāh b. al-Fawzān, 2012. He published the essay with a commentary, entitled: *al-Fawā'id al-majmū'a fī sharḥ fuṣūl al-ādāb wa makārim al-akhlāq al-mashrū'a*. The translation relied on this commentary to convey the premeditated meanings. In general, the rendition follows the system of translitera-

---

1 Paul Newmark, *A Textbook of Translation* (Hertfordshire: Prentice Hall International Ltd, 1998), 5.

2 Basil Hatim, *Discourse and the Translator* (New York: Longman, 1990), 16.

tion used in *The Encyclopaedia of Islam*. The years have been cited firstly according to the Hijrī calendar, then according to the Gregorian calendar; e.g., (d. 505/1111). Glorifications and invocations after certain names have not been included in the rendition to maintain the flow of the script. The editor's format and layout of the Arabic text is very commendable, but I did not limit myself to the editor's format while presenting the English translation, although I tried my best to maintain its foundation. In the translation, basic annotations from the commentary were included regarding the Islamic sources Ibn ʿAqīl cited. The sub-titles in bold were inserted to divide the contents of the essay. The reader should note that the opinions expressed in the translation are those of the author, and not necessarily of the translator.

Ibn ʿAqīl al-Ḥanbalī

Ibn ʿAqīl was one of the greatest scholars of Islam. He is ʿAlī b. ʿAqīl b. Muḥammad b. ʿAqīl al-Baghdadī al-Ḥanbalī; his agnomen was Abu-l-Wafāʾ. He was born in the year 431/1039. His family members from his father's side were all writers, chancery secretaries, poets, and humanists. As with many notable scholars of Islam, Ibn ʿAqīl began his quest for sacred knowledge at a very early stage of his life; he began to study law at the age of fifteen. He was born into a Ḥanafī family. Following the traditions of his family, he initially studied under the instructions of a Ḥanafī jurist, known only as Abū ʿAmr al-Faqīh. Ibn ʿAqīl studied Ḥanafī law for about a year before he transferred to the study of Ḥanbalī law. He studied Ḥanbalī law under the instruction of al-Qāḍī Abū Yaʿlā (d. 458/1066), the chief of the Ḥanbalī law school of his era. This continued until his mentor and master passed away. Both of them came from Ḥanafī families and it was probably al-Qāḍī Abū Yaʿlā's influence that caused Ibn ʿAqīl to change his law school. The biographers generally agree that Ibn ʿAqīl passed away in the year 513/1119 in Baghdad. His funeral was attended by a multitude of people.

Biographers of the past and present have praised Ibn ʿAqīl's intelligence and his contribution towards Islamic scholarship; Ibn Ḥajar al-ʿAsqalānī (d. 856/1452) said:

> This man was from amongst the greatest of scholars. Yes, he was a Muʿtazilī, but he openly repented from having such beliefs, so his repentance is accepted. He went on to author works refuting them. The scholars of his era and those after them praised Ibn ʿAqīl.

Another scholar, al-Silafī regarding Ibn ʿAqīl said:

> My eyes have not witnessed anyone similar to him. No one was able to speak (i.e. argue) with him because of his immense knowledge,

> eloquence, appropriateness of his inclusions, and the strength of his arguments.[3]

George Makdisi (d. 2002) studied Ibn ʿAqīl's life in great detail and authored a very informative biography on him and his legacy. He also edited some of his important contributions in Islamic scholarship. Among the main works Makdisi edited was Ibn ʿAqīl's legal theory manual, *al-Wāḍiḥ fī uṣūl al-fiqh,* and some segments of his encyclopaedic compendium, *al-Funūn*. This compendium is believed to have included approximately 400 different subjects according to Ḥājī Khalīfa (d. 1068/1657), and reached around 200 volumes in its entire form. The historian, al-Dhahabī (d. 748/1348) considered it to be the longest ever written work. Makdisi edited two volumes from it, and the rest is said to be lost. Regarding Ibn ʿAqīl, Makdisi said:

> As I became more familiar with Ibn ʿAqīl's life, times, and thought, his place in history and his century assumed a greater significance, reaching beyond the boarders of the classical Islamic world into that of the Christian West.[4]

3 ʿAbdullāh al-Ṭurīqī, *Al-Ḥanābila khilāl thalātha ʿashar qarnā* (Beirut: 2012), vol. 3 p.216-218.

4 George Makdisi, *Ibn ʿAqil* (Edinburgh: Edinburgh University Press, 1997), xv.

Fuṣūl al-Ādāb

On the subject of Islamic manners and etiquettes, the Ḥanbalī scholars authored around twenty works; some are extant while others are believed to be lost.[5] This genre of literature varied in its style; scholars often wrote them as addendums to longer law manuals, while others preferred to do them as separate works. The works varied in length significantly, ranging from brief poems and essays to long detailed manuals. Ibn ʿAqīl's essay on Islamic manners, *Fuṣūl al-ādāb wa makārim al-akhlāq al-mashrūʿa* is one of the earlier works. The essay was written towards the end of the 5th/11th century or the beginning of the 6th/12th century. Ibn ʿAqīl divided the essay into twenty-two small sections, and includes just over one hundred and thirty different types of Islamic manners and etiquettes.

There is only one manuscript, indexed in the Laleli library, Turkey; it comprises of just six pages. The manuscript is thought to be from the 9th/15th century, a few centuries after Ibn ʿAqīl's death. The text was first edited by Dr. ʿAbd al-Salām al-Suḥaymī, and published in 2002 as a short book. Dr. ʿAbdullāh b. al-Fawzān edited it again and corrected the previous errors in al-Suḥaymī's print. This was published in 2012 with a detailed commentary, entitled: *al-Fawāʾid al-majmūʿa fī sharḥ fuṣūl al-ādāb wa makārim al-akhlāq al-mashrūʿa*. Ibn ʿAqīl's essay received other written commentaries, including: *Al-Lubāb sharḥ fuṣūl al-ādāb* and *Lubb al-lubāb mukhtaṣar sharḥ fuṣūl al-ādāb* of ʿAbdullāh b. Māniʿ al-Rūqī. In 2021 Dr. Anas al-Yatāmī and Dr. ʿAbd al-ʿAzīz al-ʿAydān authored the commentary, *Minḥa al-wahhāb bi-sharḥ fuṣūl al-ādāb*. The English translation, *Ibn ʿAqīl's Essay on Islamic Manners* relied on the 2012 Arabic edition.

Ibn ʿAqīl had another work which had a similar title, *al-Fuṣūl fī al-fiqh*. His

5 ʿAbdullāh b. Bakr Abū Zayd, *Al-Madkhal al-mufaṣṣal* (Riyadh: Dār al-ʿĀsima, 1997), vol. 2 p.609.

essay on Islamic manners might have been an addendum to this manual rather than a separate work. A number of factors allude to this although we cannot be certain. Firstly, later Ḥanbalī scholars such as Ibn Mufliḥ, al-Mardāwī, and al-Saffārīnī cited Ibn 'Aqīl in their works, but these citations and issues are not in the essay's manuscript. Secondly, the manuscript as mentioned earlier composes of only six pages, it is relatively small compared to the other contributions of Ibn 'Aqīl. Also, Ḥanbalī scholars before and after Ibn 'Aqīl often added a section on etiquettes at the end of their *fiqh* manuals.[6] This practice is apparent in Ibn Abī Mūsā's (d. 427/1036) *al-Irshād,* Ibn Ḥamdān's (d. 695/1295) *al-Ri'āya al-ṣughrā*, Ibn Balbān's (d. 1083/1672) *Mukhtaṣar al-ifādāt,* and al-Sa'dī's (d. 1376/1956) *Nūr al-baṣā'ir.* For these considerations, *Fuṣūl al-ādāb* can be argued to be a fragment of Ibn 'Aqīl's *al-Fuṣūl fī al-fiqh.*

6 'Abdullāh al-Fawzān, *Al-Fawā'id al-majmū'a* (Riyadh: Dār Ibn al-Jawzī, 2012), 7.

The Ḥanbalī school's Contribution

It was already mentioned that the Ḥanbalī school contributed abundantly to this genre of literature; however, most of the works are lost. What follows is a chronological list of Arabic Ḥanbalī texts on Islamic manners and their associated commentaries, which are available in manuscript and underwent publication. I have provided the publication details to the best of my knowledge.

- *Fuṣul al-ādāb wa makārim al-akhlāq al-mashrūʿa* of Ibn ʿAqīl (d. 513/1119). Edited by ʿAbd al-Salām al-Suḥaymī. Riyadh: Aḍwāʾ al-Salaf, 2002. This received some modern commentaries:

    Al-Fawāʾid al-majmūʿa fī sharḥ fuṣūl al-ādāb wa makārim al-akhlāq al-mashrūʿa of ʿAbdullāh b. al-Fawzān. Riyadh: Dār Ibn al-Jawzī, 2012.

    Al-Lubāb sharḥ fuṣūl al-ādāb of ʿAbdullāh b. Māniʿ al-Rūqī. Riyadh: Dār al-Tadmuriyya, 2012.

    Lubb al-lubāb mukhtaṣar sharḥ fuṣūl al-ādāb of ʿAbdullāh b. Māniʿ al-Rūqī. Riyadh: Jāmiʿ Ibn al-Qayyim.

    Minḥa al-wahhāb bi-sharḥ fuṣūl al-ādāb of Anas al-Yatāmī and ʿAbd al-ʿAzīz al-ʿAydān. Kuwait: Dār Rakāʾiz, 2021.

- *Al-Alfiyya fī al-ādāb al-sharʿīya* of Muḥammad b. ʿAbd al-Qawī al-Mardāwī (d. 699/1299). Edited by Muḥammad b. Nāṣir al-ʿAjmī. Riyadh: Dār al-Bashāʾir al-Islamiyya, 2005. This gained two classical commentaries and some contemporary ones:

    Sharḥ manẓūma al-ādāb al-sharʿīya of Mūsā al-Ḥajjāwī (d. 968/1560). Edited initially by Muḥammad al-Shuwayʿir. Riyadh: Dār Ibn al-Jawzī, 2005. Edited again by Nūr al-Dīn Ṭālib. Damascus: Dār al-Nawādir, 2012.

Ghidāʾ al-albāb li-sharḥ manẓūma al-ādāb of Muḥammad al-Saffārīnī (d. 1188/1774). The last edition by Ṣāliḥ al-Ghāmidī in six volumes. Riyadh: Dār al-Bashāʾir al-Islamiyya, 2017.

Itḥāf al-ṭullāb bi-sharḥ manẓūma al-ādāb of Ṣāliḥ al-Fawzān. Riyadh: Maktaba al-Rushd, 2014.

- *Al-Ādāb al-sharʿīya* of Muḥammad b. Mufliḥ (d. 763/1362). Edited by Shuʿayb al-Arnāʾūṭ in four volumes. Beirut: Muʾassasa al-Risāla, 2012.

فصول الآداب

ومكارم الأخلاق المشروعة

تأليف

الإمام العلامة أبي الوفاء علي بن عقيل بن محمد
ابن عقيل بن عبد الله البغدادي الظفري
المتوفى سنة ٥١٣ هـ

[Introduction]

In the name of Allāh, the Gracious, the Merciful

My Lord, make it easy and not difficult.

All praise belongs to Allāh, the Lord of the worlds. May Allāh's abundant blessings and peace be upon Muḥammad, the last of the prophets, and leader of the righteous; may Allāh's blessing be upon his household and his companions until the Day of Judgment. This is a fragment from the chapters in Islamic manners and praiseworthy etiquettes authored by the honorable Imām, Abū l-Wafā' b. 'Aqīl – may Allāh have mercy on him.

Greetings (*salām*)

The walking person initiates the greeting for the seated person and the person in a vehicle initiates the greeting for those walking or sitting. It is recommended to initiate the greeting.

If a person gave the greeting from a group of walking people or from a group of people in a vehicle, the greeting of that single person will suffice on behalf of that group. Similarly, if only a person from a group of seated people replied to the greeting, it will suffice on behalf of that group.

The formula for the greeting is: *salāmun 'alaykum*, and the reply is: *wa-'alaykum al-salām*. The extra phrase recommended to be added is: *wa-raḥmatullāh wa-barakātu*. It is not recommended to add beyond these phrases in the greeting. It is recommended for the one initiating the greeting to limit it to: *salāmun 'alaykum wa-raḥmatullāh* because this will allow the replying person to answer with a better phrase than the initiator of the greeting.

[مقدمة]

بسم الله الرحمن الرحيم

رَبِّ يَسِّرْ وَلَا تُعَسِّرْ

الحَمْدُ للهِ رَبِّ العَالَمِينَ، وصَلَّى اللَّهُ عَلَى مُحَمَّدٍ خاتَمِ النَّبِيِّيْنَ وَإِمَامِ المُتَّقِينَ، وَعَلَى آلِهِ وَصَحْبِهِ أَجْمَعِيْنَ، وَسَلَّمَ تَسْلِيْمًا كَثِيْرًا إِلَى يَوْمِ الدِّيْنِ. هَذِهِ نُبْذَةٌ مِنْ فُصُوْلِ الآدَابِ وَمَكَارِمِ الأَخْلَاقِ المَشْرُوْعَةِ مِنْ تَأْلِيفِ الشَّيْخِ الإِمَامِ القُدْوَةِ أَبِي الوَفَاءِ ابنِ عَقِيلٍ رحمه الله تعالى.

فَصْلٌ

السَّلَامُ المُبْتَدَأُ يَكُوْنُ مِنَ المَاشِي عَلَى القَاعِدِ، وَمِنَ الرَّاكِبِ عَلَى المَاشِي وَالجَالِسِ، وَالابْتِدَاءُ بِهِ سُنَّةٌ.

وَإِذَا سَلَّمَ الوَاحِدُ مِنَ الجَمَاعَةِ المُشَاةِ أَوِ الرُّكَّابِ أَجْزَأَ عَنِ الجَمَاعَةِ، وَإِذَا رَدَّ وَاحِدٌ مِنَ الجَمَاعَةِ مِنَ الجُلُوسِ أَجْزَأَ عَنِ الجَمَاعَةِ.

وَصِفَةُ السَّلَامِ: سَلَامٌ عَلَيْكُم، وَصِفَةُ الرَّدِّ: وَعَلَيْكُمُ السَّلَامُ، وَالزِّيَادَةُ المَأْمُوْرُ بِهَا المُسْتَحَبَّةُ: وَرَحْمَةُ اللهِ وَبَرَكَاتُهُ، وَلَا يُسْتَحَبُّ الزِّيَادَةُ عَلَى ذَلِكَ. وَيُسْتَحَبُّ لِلْمُسَلِّمِ أَنْ يَقْتَصِرَ على قَولِ: سَلَامٌ عَلَيْكُمْ وَرَحْمَةُ اللهِ، لِيَتْرُكَ لِلْمُجِيْبِ الزِّيَادَةَ المَأْمُوْرَ بِهَا - وَهِيَ قَوْلُهُ: وَبَرَكَاتُهُ - بِأَحْسَنَ مِنْهَا أَوْ رُدُّوهَا.

If something separated two individuals after greeting each other such as a tree or a wall, then repeating the greeting upon meeting each other again is recommended. The Companions of the Prophet used to do this.

It is reprehensible to give the greeting to young women. Giving greetings to them necessitates a reply and listening to their voices which can lead to temptations. Is it not so that many voices have lead people to temptations and passion? There is no problem giving greetings to senile women and women who openly deal with men as there is no notion of temptation from hearing their voices. Out of necessity, the women who openly deal with men require the greeting to be given to her and similarly, the acceptance of her reply.

It is permissible for a witness to look at a woman's face so as to memorise her features and establish the witnessing. Similarly, it is permissible for gold-smiths, spinners of wool or anyone else to look at the face of women, who do business with women in the trading industry.

There is no problem greeting children to teach them manners which make it beloved to them and accustom them to good social practices.

It is recommended to do the greeting when encountering and departing from a person. However, it is more strongly recommended to do the greeting when encountering.

Shaking hands, hugging, kissing and standing up for others

It is recommended for men to shake hands. However, it is not permissible for men to shake the hands of young women as this will arouse temptations and desires.

There are no problems in hugging a person. Likewise, it is permissible to kiss the head or the hand of those of religiosity, knowledge, or an advanced

وَإِذَا سَلَّمَ ثُمَّ حَالَ بَيْنَهُ وَبَيْنَ مَنْ سَلَّمَ عَلَيْهِ شَجَرَةٌ أَوْ جِدَارٌ ثُمَّ الْتَقَوْا عَادَتْ سُنَّةُ السَّلَامِ، كَذَلِكَ كَانَ أَصْحَابُ النَّبِيِّ ﷺ وَرَضِيَ عَنْهُم.

وَيُكْرَهُ السَّلَامُ عَلَى شَوَابِّ النِّسَاءِ، فَإِنَّ ذَلِكَ يَجْلِبُ جَوَابَهُنَّ، وَسمَاع أَصْوَاتِهِنَّ، وَعَسَاهُ يَجْلُبُ الفِتْنَةَ، وَكَمْ مِنْ صَوْتٍ جَرَّ هَوًى وَعِشْقًا، وَلَا بَأسَ بِالسَّلَامِ عَلَى العَجَائِزِ وَالبَارِزَاتِ لِعَدَمِ الفِتنَةِ بِأَصْوَاتِهِنَّ، وَلِأَنَّ البَرْزَةَ تَحْتَاجُ إِلَى السَّلَامِ عَلَيْهَا وَرَدِّ سَلَامِهَا.

وَلِلْحَاجَةِ تَأْثِيرٌ بِذَلِكَ لِجَوَازِ النَّظَرِ إِلَى وَجْهِ المَرْأَةِ لِلشَّاهِدِ لِيَحْفَظَ الحِلْيَةَ فَيُقِيمَ الشَّهَادَةَ، وَكَذَلِكَ الصَّائِغُ وَالمَغَازِلِيُّ، وَكُلُّ مَنْ تُعَامِلُهُ النِّسَاءُ مِنْ أَرْبَابِ التَّجَائِرِ وَالصَّنَائِعِ.

وَلَا بَأْسَ بِالسَّلَامِ عَلَى الصِّبْيَانِ تَعْلِيمًا لَهُمْ لِلْأَدَبِ، وَتَحْبِيبًا لِحُسْنِ الخُلُقِ، وَتَدْرِيبًا وتَمْرِينًا عَلَى حُسْنِ المُعَاشَرَةِ.

وَيَسْتَحَبُّ السَّلَامُ عِنْدَ الإِنْصِرَافِ كَمَا يُسْتَحَبُّ عِنْدَ الدُّخُوْلِ، وَالدُّخُوْلُ أَشَدُّ اِسْتِحْبَابًا.

فَصْلٌ

وَالمُصَافَحَةٌ مُسْتَحَبَّةٌ بَيْنَ الرَّجُلَينِ. وَلَا تَجُوْزُ مُصَافَحَةُ النِّسَاءِ الشَّوَابِّ؛ لِأَنَّ ذَلِكَ يُثِيرُ الشَّهْوَةَ.

وَلَا بَأسَ بِالْمُعَانَقَةِ، وَتَقْبِيلِ الرَّأْسِ وَاليَدِ، لِمَنْ يَكُوْنُ مِنْ أَهْلِ الدِّيْنِ

age [spent] in Islam.

It is recommended to stand up for just rulers, parents, and religious personalities, that is, personalities of piety and knowledge and individuals of noble nature and descent. Besides the aforementioned, it is not recommended to stand for anyone else.

Listening to private conversations

It is not befitting for a person to get into people's secrets or conversations that others did not include him in. It is not permissible to listen to the consultations of a group of people.

If a person keeps looking around during a conversation, this should be treated as a private conversation. In this scenario it becomes obligatory to safeguard the person's words because him looking around suggests that he is worried about people listening to his conversation.

Walking arrogantly

It is reprehensible to walk arrogantly; a person should walk moderately. Walking arrogantly is hateful to Allāh, however it is not hateful when a person walks arrogantly in front of enemy lines.

Shortcomings of people

It is from noble manners to ignore any shortcomings of people, and that which emanates from heedlessness such as exposure of *ʿawra* (nakedness) and the release of gas accompanied by sound or smell. Whoever hears it should appear not to hear it, pretend to be asleep or ignore it to avoid the

أَوِ العِلْمِ أَوِ كِبَرِ السِّنِّ فِي الإِسْلَامِ.

وَيُسْتَحَبُّ القِيَامُ لِلإِمَامِ العَادِلِ، وَالوَالِدَيْنِ، وَأَهْلِ الدِّيْنِ وَالوَرَعِ وَالعِلْمِ وَالكَرَمِ وَالنَّسَبِ، وَلَا يُسْتَحَبُّ لِغَيْرِ هَؤُلَاءِ.

فَصْلٌ

وَيَنْبَغِي لِلإِنْسَانِ أَنْ لَا يَدْخُلَ فِي سِرِّ قَوْمٍ، وَلَا حَدِيْثٍ لَمْ يُدْخِلُوْهُ فِيْهِ. وَلَا يَجُوْزُ الاسْتِمَاعُ إِلَى كَلَامِ قَوْمٍ يَتَشَاوَرُوْنَ.

وَمَنْ تَلَفَّتَ فِي حَدِيثِهِ فَهُوَ كَالمُسْتَوْدِعِ لِحَدِيْثِهِ، يَجِبُ حِفْظُهُ عَلَيْهِ؛ لِأَنَّ تَلَفُّتَهُ يُعْطِي التَّفَلُّتَ وَالتَّفَزُّعَ.

فَصْلٌ

وَيُكْرَهُ الخُيَلَاءُ، وَالزَّهْوُ فِي المَشْيِ، وَإِنَّمَا يَمْشِيْ قَصْدًا، فَإِنَّ الخُيَلَاءَ مِشْيَةٌ يُبْغِضُهَا اللهُ تَعَالَى؛ إِلَّا بَيْنَ الصَّفَّيْنِ.

فَصْلٌ

ومِنْ مَكَارِمِ الأَخْلَاقِ التَّغَافُلُ عَنْ ظُهورِ مَسَاوِئِ النَّاسِ وَمَا يبدُو فِي غَفلاتِهِمْ مِنْ كَشْفِ عورَةٍ، أَو خُرُوجِ رِيح لَهَا صَوْتٌ، أَوْ رِيْحٌ، وَمَنْ سَمِعَ ذَلِكَ فأظْهَرَ الطَّرَشَ أَوِ النَّومَ أَوِ الغَفْلَةَ لِيُزِيْلَ خَجَلَ الفَاعِلِ كَانَ

person from getting embarrassed. This is from noble etiquettes.

Natural disposition

Ten things are natural for a person to do; five pertaining to the head and five things pertaining to rest of the body. Snuffing water, rinsing the mouth, using the tooth stick, trimming the moustache and growing the beard pertain to the head. Removing the pubic and armpit hairs, clipping the nails, using water to clean the private parts, and performing the circumcision all relate to the body.

White hair

It is reprehensible to pluck out white hair strands because it has been reported in a ḥadīth that the white hair 'is Allāh's light'.[2] The growth of white hair also warns a person of his death, reduces his hopes in life, encourages him to do righteous actions, and it makes a person dignified. It is reprehensible to shave the back of the head unless a person intends to do bloodlettings as mentioned in the books of ḥadīth (i.e. shave part of the head and leave part of it).

Permission to enter a person's residence

It is not befitting to enter into a person's residence without their permission, whether the person was a relative or someone foreign. This is to avoid catching people in inappropriate clothing that may expose their *ʿawra* (nakedness). Permission is requested three times. If permission is granted, the person can enter but without permission, the person should not enter.

2 The report presented by Ibn ʿAqīl is worded slightly different in the books of ḥadīth: *Abū Dāwūd* (4202); *al-Tirmidhī* (2721); *Ibn Māja* (3721) and others. The editor mentioned that he was not able to find the report Ibn ʿAqīl mentioned with these specific wordings.

ذَلِكَ مِنْ مَكَارِمِ الأَخْلَاقِ.

فَصْلٌ

وَعَشَرَةٌ مِنَ الفِطْرَةِ، خَمْسٌ فِي الرَّأْسِ، وَخَمْسٌ فِي الجَسَدِ. فَالَّتِي فِيْ الرَّأس: الْمَضْمَضَةُ، وَالاسْتِنْشَاقُ، وَالسِّوَاكُ، وَقَصُّ الشَّارِبِ، وَإِعْفَاءُ اللِّحْيَةِ. وَالَّتِيْ فِي الجَسَدِ: حَلْقُ العَانَةِ، وَنَتْفُ الإِبِطَيْنِ، وَتَقْلِيْمُ الأَظْفَارِ، وَالاسْتِنْجَاءُ، وَالخِتَانُ.

فَصْلٌ

وَيُكْرَهُ نَتْفُ الشَّيْبِ، فَقَدْ وَرَدَ فِي الْحَدِيْثِ «**أَنَّهُ نُوْرُ اللهِ**»، وَهُوَ أَيْضًا نَذِيْرُ الْمَوْتِ، وَيُقَصِّرُ الأَمَلَ، وَحَاثٌ عَلَى حُسْنِ العَمَلِ، وَوَقَارٌ. وَيُكْرَهُ حَلْقُ القَفَا؛ إِلا لِمَنْ أَرَادَ الحِجَامَةَ، كَذَلِكَ رُوِيَ فِي السُّنَنِ.

فَصْلٌ

وَلَا يَنْبَغِي لِأَحَدٍ أَنْ يَهْجُمَ عَلَى أَقَارِبَ، أَوْ أَجَانِبَ؛ لِئَلَّا يُصَادِفَ بَذْلَةً مِنْ كَشْفِ عَوْرَةٍ، وَيَسْتَأْذِنُ ثلاثًا، فَإِنْ أُذِنَ لَهُ وَإِلَّا رَجَعَ.

Private conversations

It is prohibited for two people to have a private conversation excluding a third person (who is present among them). This necessitates desolation (i.e. displeasure) and affects a person's heart.

Eating and drinking

When a person commences eating, it is recommended to say, *bismillāh,* and when one ends, it is recommended to say, *al-ḥamdulillāh*. The person should eat with his right hand. If the food was of one type, the person should eat what is nearest to him (i.e. in front of him).

A person should not eat from the centre of a dish (i.e. the highest part), but should start from its sides. Likewise, when weighing foodstuff, a person should not start from the centre. This is done to receive blessings as reported in the Prophetic traditions.

A person should not blow on hot or cold food. It is not reprehensible to eat and drink standing but it is reprehensible while reclining. If a person finished with some food or drink and needs to pass it on, the person should start with the individual on his right first – this is what the Prophet used to do.

Bedtime

Before sleeping a person should lock his doors, seal water bottles, cover utensils, and turn off the lights – as narrated in the Prophetic traditions.

Aḥmad b. Ḥanbal reprehended the washing of hands before eating food. However, there is a report regarding washing the hands for food, perhaps Aḥmad did not consider this report to be authentic.

فَصْلٌ

وَيَحْرُمُ أَنْ يَتَنَاجَا اثْنَانِ دُوْنَ ثَالِثٍ؛ لِأَنَّهُ يُوْجِبُ إِيْحَاشًا، وَكَسْرَ الْقَلْبِ.

۞

فَصْلٌ

وَيُسْتَحَبُّ اِفْتِتَاحُ الأَكْلِ بِبِسْمِ اللهِ، وَخَتْمُهُ بِالحَمْدُ للهِ، وَأَنْ يَأْكُلَ بِيَمِيْنِهِ، مِمَّا يَلِيْهِ، إِذَا كَانَ الطعَامُ نَوْعًا وَاحِدًا.

وَلَا يَأْكُلُ مِنْ ذِرْوَةِ الطَّعَامِ لَكِنْ مِنْ جَوَانِبِهِ. وَكَذَلِكَ الكَيْلُ، فَإِنَّهُ أَدْعَى لِلْبَرَكَةِ، كَذَلِكَ رُوِيَ فِي السُّنَنِ.

وَلَا يَنْفَخُ فِي الطَّعَامَ الحَارِّ وَلَا البَارِدِ، وَلَا يُكْرَهُ الأَكْلُ والشُّرْبُ قَائِمًا، وَيُكْرَهُ مُتَّكِئًا. وَإِذَا أَرَادَ دَفْعَ إِنَاءِ الشَّرَابِ أَوِ اللُّقْمَةِ، دَفَعَ إِلَى مَنْ عَنْ يَمِيْنِهِ أَوَّلا، كَذَلِكَ كَانَ يَفْعَلُ النَّبِيُّ ﷺ.

۞

فَصْلٌ

وَمَنْ أَرَادَ النَّوْمَ يُغْلِقُ بَابَهُ، وَيُوْكِي سِقَاءَهُ، وَيُغَطِّي إِنَاءَهُ، وَيُطْفِئُ سِرَاجَهُ، كَذَلِكَ رُوِيَ فِي السُّنَنِ عَنِ النَّبِيِّ ﷺ.

وَكَرِهَ أَحْمَدُ رضي الله عنه غَسْلَ اليَدِ لِلطَّعَامِ، وَقَدْ وَرَدَ فِي الخَبَرِ غَسْلُ اليَدِ لَهُ، وَلَعَلهُ مَا صَحَّ عِنْدَ أَحْمَدَ رضي الله عنه.

Strong odours, mosques, invitations, and rights of a Muslim

It is recommended to wash hands immediately after eating food that has strong odours. And it is strongly recommended to wash them before sleep because there is a report condemning individuals who do not wash hands before sleeping, due to vermin.

Whoever enters the mosque for praying or for devotional seclusion, it is reprehensible for such a person to consume unpleasant vegetables such as onions, garlic, and leek. The Prophet forbade from nearing the mosques after eating such vegetables.

It is recommended to accept wedding feast invitations. It is not necessary for a person to accept invitations for circumcision ceremonies – this is something new in Islam. If a person attends for a wedding feast, it is not incumbent for him to eat the food. The person can eat if he wants, however he should make himself present, supplicate for the person, and then leave if he wants.

It is recommended to go to invitations which are free from play, amusement, and evil. However, it is prohibited to attend gatherings containing prohibited elements. If it contains reprehensible elements, the ruling for attending such a gathering will be reprehensible.

It is reprehensible for the people of nobility and virtue to readily accept food invitations. They should excuse themselves from attending non-Islamic gatherings. By attending such gatherings it can abase a person and reduce people's reverence for them.

The following things are recommended for a Muslim to do: visit his sick Muslim brother, attend his funeral, and send condolences to his family. A non-Muslim citizen can be visited during his illness. The Prophet visited a sick Jew and said: **"How are you doing O Jew?"**[3]

3 The editor mentioned that he was not able to find the report Ibn ʿAqīl mentioned with these specific wordings. However, Ibn al-Qayyim mentioned a report in his book, *Aḥkām ahl al-dhimma,* (vol.1 p. 202) which resembles its wordings.

فَصْلٌ

وَيُسْتَحَبُّ تَحْوِيْلُ غَسْلِ اليَدِ مِنَ الزُّهَامِ، وَعِنْدَ النَّوْمِ أَشَدُّ اِسْتِحْبَابًا، فَقَدْ وَرَدَ التَّحْذِيْرُ مِنْهُ، لِأَجْلِ الهَوَامِّ.

وَيُكْرَهُ لِمَنْ أَرَادَ الْمَسَاجِدَ لِلصَّلَاةِ وَالاعتِكَافِ أَنْ يَتعَرَّضَ لِأَكْلِ الخَبَائِثِ مِنَ البُقُوْلِ؛ كَالبَصَلِ وَالثُّوْمِ وَالكُرَّاثِ، فَقَدْ نَهَى النبيُّ ﷺ عَنْ قُرْبَانِ الْمَسْجِدِ مَعَهُ.

وَيُسْتَحَبُّ الإِجَابَةُ إِلَى وَلِيْمَةِ العُرْسِ، وَلَيْسَ عَلَيْهِ أَنْ يَسْتَجِيْبَ إِلَى وَلِيْمَةِ الخِتَانِ؛ فَإِنَّهَا مُحْدَثَةٌ. وَإِذَا حَضَرَ وَلِيْمَةَ العُرْسِ لَمْ يَكُنْ عَلَيْهِ الأَكْلُ، بَلْ إِنْ أَكَلَ وَإِلَّا دَعَا وَانْصَرَفَ.

وَإِنَّمَا يُسْتَحَبُّ الإِجَابَةُ إِلَيْهَا إِذَا لَمْ يَكُنْ فِيْهَا لَعِبٌ وَلَا مُنْكَرٌ وَلَا لَهْوٌ، فَإِنْ كَانَ فِيْهَا مُحَرَّمٌ حَرُمَتِ الإِجَابَةُ، وَإِنْ كَانَ فِيْهَا مَكْرُوْهٌ كُرِهَتِ الإِجَابَةُ.

وَيُكْرَهُ لِأَهْلِ المُرُوْءَاتِ وَالفَضَائِلِ التَسَرُّعُ إِلَى إِجَابَةِ الطَّعَامِ، وَالتَّسَامُحُ بِحُضُوْرِ الوَلَائِمِ غَيرِ الشَّرْعِيَّةِ، فَإِنَّهُ يُوْرِثُ دَنَاءَةً، وَإِسْقَاطَ الهَيْبَةِ مِنْ صُدُوْرِ النَّاسِ.

وَيُسْتَحَبُّ لِلْمُسْلِمِ عِيَادَةُ أَخِيْهِ المُسْلِمِ، وَحُضُوْرُ جَنَازَتِهِ إِذَا مَاتَ، وَتَعْزِيَةُ أَهْلِهِ. وَلَا بَأْسَ بِعِيَادَةِ الذِّمِّيِّ، فَقَدْ عَادَ النَّبِيُّ ﷺ يَهُوْدِيًّا، وَقَالَ: «**كَيْفَ تَجِدُكَ يَا يَهُوْدِيُّ؟**».

Backbiting

It is prohibited to backbite a person who conceals his sins and shameful deeds. Allāh said: "Do not backbite each other."[4]

If an evil person is mentioned to warn others, this will not be considered as backbiting. A person can speak the truth about an evil person when enquired for marriage proposals, business partnerships, and social dealings. The person who speaks about the evil individual (i.e. to warn others) will not be sinful but will be rewarded for being honest. The Prophet said: **"Say regarding the evil person which will warn others of him."**[5]

'Umar was not considered to have fallen into backbiting when he mentioned some of the faults and weaknesses of the committee members when consulting about who should succeed him. 'Umar mentioned their faults and weaknesses for the sake of Allāh, His messenger, and Islam.

Subsection

Backbiting occurs when a person's shortcomings and ills are mentioned; it is done to undermine the person.

It is recommended to control one's tongue, and speak little unless it is really necessary. It is better to use the tongue to benefit oneself and others than to remain silent. This includes reading the Qur'ān, teaching knowledge, remembering Allāh, commanding good, forbidding evil, and making peace between people.

4 Qur'ān 49:12

5 There is another narration with a different wording in *Kashf al-khafā'* (vol. 1 p.114), but the report is not authentic.

فَصْلٌ

وَالغِيْبَةُ حَرَامٌ فِي حَقِّ مَنْ لَمْ يَنْكَشِفْ بِالمَعَاصِي وَالقَبَائِحِ، لِقَوْلِهِ تَعَالَى: ﴿وَلَا يَغْتَب بَّعْضُكُم بَعْضًا﴾ الآية.

وَمَنْ ذَكَرَ فِي فَاسِقٍ مَا فِيْهِ لِيُحْذَرَ مِنْهُ أَوْ سَأَلَ عَنْهُ مَنْ يُرِيْدُ تَزْوِيْجَهُ أَوْ شَرِكَتَهُ أَوْ مُعَامِلَتَهُ لَمْ يَكُنْ مُغْتَابًا لَهُ، وَلَا عَلَيْهِ إِثْمُ الغِيْبَةِ، وَلَهُ ثَوَابُ النَّصِيْحَةِ، لِقَوْلِ النَّبِيِّ ﷺ: «**قُوْلُوا فِي الفَاسِقِ مَا فِيْهِ يَحْذَرْهُ النَّاسُ**».

وَلَا يُظَنُّ بِعُمَرَ رضي الله عنه أَنَّهُ أَقْدَمَ عَلَى مَا هُوَ غِيْبَةٌ عِنْدَ نَصِّهِ عَلَى السِّتَّةِ وَجَعْلِ الشُّوْرَى فِيْهِم، حَيْثُ ذَكَرَ عَيْبَ كُلِّ وَاحِدٍ، بَلْ قَصَدَ بِذَلِكَ النُّصْحَ لِلّهِ وَلِرَسُوْلِهِ وَلِأَهْلِ الإِسْلَامِ.

فَصْلٌ

فَصَارَتِ الغِيْبَةُ مَا يُذْكَرُ مِنَ النَّقْصِ وَالعَيْبِ لَا يُقْصَدُ بِهِ إِلَّا الإِزْرَاءُ عَلَى المَذْكُوْرِ، وَالطَّعْنُ فِيْهِ.

وَيُسْتَحَبُّ ضَبْطُ الأَلْسِنَةِ وَحِفْظُهَا، وَالإِقْلَالُ مِنَ الكَلَامِ إِلَّا فِيْمَا يَعْنِي وَلَا بُدَّ مِنْهُ. وَأَفْضَلُ مِنَ الصَّمْتِ إِجْرَاءُ الأَلْسِنَةِ بِمَا فِيْهِ النَّفْعُ لِغَيْرِهِ، وَالانْتِفَاعُ لِنَفْسِهِ، مِثْلُ قَوْلِهِ القُرْآنَ، وَتَدْرِيْسِ العِلْمِ، وَذِكْرِ اللّهِ تَعَالَى، وَالأَمْرِ بِالمَعْرُوْفِ، وَالنَّهْيِ عَنِ المُنْكَرِ، وَالإِصْلَاحِ بَيْنَ النَّاسِ.

Clothing and beatification

Silk clothing is prohibited for men and permissible for women. This is also the case with gold jewellery. It is prohibited for men to wear rings containing gold even if it contained an insignificant amount of it.

It is not reprehensible to wear silk garments that are mixed with animal fur; however, the fur content must be more than the silk content. Similarly, garments with more cotton content than silk are not reprehensible for men to wear.

It is not permissible to have pictures on clothes nor is it permissible to have it on beddings and curtains; the prohibition pertains to images of living beings. This is owing to the Prophetic report; **"Angels do not enter a house, which has pictures in it."**[6]

It is better to wear rings on the left hand however if a person wears it on his right hand, it is not a problem.

It is not permissible for anyone to drag his garments out of pride and arrogance.

It is permissible for men to use public baths as long as they cover the lower parts of their body (i.e. *'awra*). However, it is reprehensible for women to use public baths unless there is an excuse or a pressing need.

There is no harm in colouring one's hair with Henna, in fact it is recommended. It is also recommended to colour it using Katam, however it is reprehensible to colour one's hair black.

It is not permissible for a man to be in seclusion with a marriageable woman. It is also impermissible for two nude males or two females to share one duvet or a single lower garment.

It is impermissible to purposefully attend gatherings of play and amusement, nor those which have musical instruments such as drums and wind-based instruments. The play of the duff has been singled out for weddings. This is because of the Prophetic report, **"Announce the marriage to oth-**

6 This alludes to the ḥadīth in *Ṣaḥīḥ al-Bukhārī* (5949) and *Ṣaḥīḥ Muslim* (2106)

فَصْلٌ

وَلُبسُ الحَرِيْرِ مُحَرَّمٌ عَلَى الرِّجَالِ، مُبَاحٌ لِلنِّسَاءِ، وَكَذَلِكَ التَحلِّي بِالذَّهَبِ حَتَّى الخَاتَمِ، وَلَو بِقَدْرِ عَيْنِ الجَرَادَةِ.

وَلَا يُكرَهُ لُبسُ الخزِّ الَّذِي يَشُوْبُهُ الوَبَرُ، ويَكُونُ الوَبَرُ أَكْثَرَ، وَكَذَلِكَ العُتَابِيُّ الَّذِيْ يَكُوْنُ القُطْنُ فِيْهِ أَكْثَرَ مِنَ القَزِّ.

وَلَا يَجُوْزُ جَعْلُ الصُّوَرِ فِي الثِّيَابِ، وَلَا المَفَارِشِ وَالسُّتُوْرِ، وَهُوَ مَا كَانَ عَلَى صُوْرَةِ حَيَوَانٍ، لِأَنَّ النَّبِيَّ ﷺ قَالَ: «**لَا تَدْخُلُ المَلَائِكَةُ بَيْتًا فِيْهِ صُوْرَةٌ**».

وَالاخْتِيَارُ التَختُّمُ فِي اليَسَارِ، وَإِنْ تَختَّمَ فِي اليَمِيْنِ فَلَا بَأْسَ.

وَلَا يَحِلُّ لِأَحَدٍ أَنْ يَجُرَّ ثَوْبَهُ خُيَلَاءَ وَبَطَرًا.

وَدُخُوْلُ الحَمَّامِ جَائِزٌ لِلرِّجَالِ بِالمَيَازِرِ السَّاتِرَةِ، وَيُكْرَهُ لِلنِّسَاءِ إِلَّا مِنْ عِلَّةٍ وَحَاجَةٍ.

وَلَا بَأْسَ بِالخِضَابِ بِالحِنَّاءِ، وَهُوَ يُسْتَحَبُّ، وَكَذَلِكَ الكَتَمُ، وَيُكْرَهُ بِالسَّوَادِ.

وَلَا يَجُوْزُ أَنْ يَخْلُوَ الرَّجُلُ بِامْرَأَةٍ لَيْسَتْ لَهُ بِمَحْرَمٍ. وَلَا يَجْتَمِعُ رَجُلَانِ، وَلَا امْرَأَتَانِ عَرْيَانَيْنِ، فِي فِرَاشٍ وَاحِدٍ وَلَا إِزَارٍ وَاحِدٍ.

وَلَا يَجُوْزُ تَعَمُّدُ حُضُوْرِ اللَّهْوِ وَاللَّعِبِ، وَلَا شَيْءٍ مِنَ المَلَاهِي المُطْرِبَةِ كَالطَّبْلِ، وَالزَّمْرِ. وَخُصَّ مِنْ ذَلِكَ الدُّفُّ لِلنِّكَاحِ؛ لِقَوْلِ النَّبِيِّ ﷺ:

ers and play the duff."[7]

There is no harm in using Allāh's names to protect oneself and to use it in amulets (*taʿwīdh*).

Medical treatments

Treating illnesses through cupping, venesection, cauterization, and intake of medicine is permissible. However, it is impermissible to treat illnesses with prohibited and impure things. It has been narrated from Aḥmad that he considered venesection and cauterization to be reprehensible, but the other narration from Aḥmad is believed to be more authentic.

Pests

If a person sees a snake in his house, he should command it to leave three times, and if it reappears, he should kill the snake. Aḥmad said: "If the snake was a *Dhu al-Ṭufyatayn* or an *al-Abtar*, it can be killed. The person does not need to command it to leave before killing such snakes." *Dhu al-Ṭufyatayn* is a snake that has two black stripes on its back and *al-Abtar* is a short tailed snake. The way to command a snake to leave from one's residence is as follows: 'Pass by in peace!' or 'Leave in peace!'

It is permissible to kills geckos but it's impermissible to kill ants or destroy their nests. It is reprehensible to kill lice using fire and it is impermissible to kill frogs because the Prophet forbade the killing of frogs.

7 Reported in *Mustadrak al-Ḥākim* vol.2 p. 173

«أَعْلِنُوا النِّكَاحَ وَاضْرِبُوْا عَلَيْهِ بِالدُّفِّ».

وَلَا بَأسَ بِأَسْمَاءِ اللّٰهِ تَعَالَى، وَكَذَلِكَ التَعْوِيْذُ بِهِ.

فَصْلٌ

وَالتَّدَاوِيْ بِالحِجَامَةِ، وَالفَصْدِ، وَالكَيِّ، وَشُرْبِ الأَدْوِيَةِ جَائِزٌ، وَلَا يَجُوزُ التَدَاوِيْ بِمُحَرَّمٍ وَلَا نَجِسٍ، وَقَدْ رُوِيَ عَنْ أَحْمَدَ كَرَاهِيَّةُ الكَيِّ، وَقَطْعِ العُرُوْقِ، وَالرِّوَايَةُ الأُوْلَى أَصَحُّ.

فَصْلٌ

وَمَنْ رَأَى مِنَ الحَيَّاتِ شَيْئًا فِي مَنْزِلِهِ فَلْيُؤْذِنْهُ ثَلَاثًا، إِنْ بَدَا لَهُ بَعْدَ ذَلِكَ قَتَلَهُ، وَقَدْ قَالَ الإِمَامُ أَحْمَدُ ﵁: إِنْ كَانَ ذُو الطُّفْيَتَيْنِ وَالأَبْتَرُ قَتَلَهُ، وَلَمْ يُؤْذِنْهُ، وَذُوْ الطُّفْيَتَيْنِ: الَّذِي بِظَهْرِهِ خَطٌّ أَسْوَدُ، وَالأَبْتَرُ: الغَلِيْظُ القَصِيْرُ الذَّنَبِ. وَصِفَةُ القَوْلِ الَّذِيْ يُؤْذِنُهُ: امْضِ بِسَلَامٍ، أَوِ اذْهَبْ بِسَلَامٍ.

وَيَجُوْزُ قَتْلُ الأَوْزَاغِ، وَلَا يَجُوْزُ قَتْلُ النَّمْلِ وَلَا تَخْرِيْبُ أَجْحُرَتِهِنَّ، وَيُكْرَهُ قَتْلُ القَمْلِ بِالنَّارِ. وَلَا يَحِلُّ قَتْلُ الضَفَادِعِ؛ لِأَنَّ النَّبِيَّ ﷺ نَهَى عَنْ قَتْلِ الضِّفْدَعِ.

Etiquettes in the mosques

It is reprehensible to remove bodily-filth inside mosques; actions such as clipping nails, trimming moustaches, and removing armpit hairs are therefore reprehensible. Similarly, it is reprehensible to use mosques for labour and craftworks. Actions such as embroidery, needlework, ginning cotton, trading, and similar actions are therefore reprehensible if carried out abundantly. However, if the craftworks are insignificant, it will not be reprehensible. So, actions such as patching one's garment, mending one's sandals, and fixing one of its straps that came apart are not reprehensible.

Treatment of livestock animals

It is impermissible to castrate livestock animals and brand them using a hot source. However, it is permissible to do the latter for treatments, that is, only to an extent it is permitted for people to be treated. This is according to one of the opinions of Imām Aḥmad.

Parents

Good treatment of one's parents is incumbent upon a person (*wājib*). Imām Aḥmad was asked regarding good treatment of one's parents, he replied, "I do not say it is obligatory (*farḍ*) but its incumbent upon a person (*wājib*)."

It is not permissible to obey them while disobeying Allāh; it has been narrated from Aḥmad in this manner because of the Prophetic report: **"There is no obedience to the creation in disobedience to Allāh."**[8]

8 There are similar reports to this one in *Ṣaḥīḥ Muslim* (1840 and 1839)

فَصْلٌ

وَيُكْرَهُ إِزَالَةُ الأَوْسَاخِ فِي الْمَسَاجِدِ؛ كَتَقْلِيْمِ الأَظْفَارِ، وَقَصِّ الشَّارِبِ، وَنَتْفِ الإِبِطِ، وَالعَمَلُ وَالصَّنَائِعُ؛ كَالخِيَاطَةِ وَالخَرزِ، وَالحَلَجِ، وَالتِّجَارَةِ، وَمَا شَاكَلَ ذَلِكَ إِذَا كَثُرَ، وَلَا يُكْرَهُ ذَلِكَ إِذَا قَلَّ مِثْلُ رَقعِ ثَوْبٍ، أَوْ خَصْفِ نَعْلٍ، أَوْ تَشْرِيْكِهَا إِذَا انْقَطَعَ شِسْعُهَا.

فَصْلٌ

وَلَا يَجُوْزُ إِخْصَاءُ البَهَائِمِ، وَلَا كَيُّهَا بِالنَّارِ لِلْوَسْمِ، وَتَجُوْزُ المُدَاوَاةُ حَسْبَ ما أَجَزْنَا فِي حَقِّ النَّاسِ فِي إِحْدَى الرِّوَايَتَيْنِ.

فَصْلٌ

وَبِرُّ الوَالِدَيْنِ وَاجِبٌ، سُئِلَ أَحْمَدُ ﵁ عَنْ بِرِّ الوَالِدَيْنِ أَفَرْضٌ هُوَ؟ فَقَالَ: لَا أَقُوْلُ فَرْضٌ، وَلَكِنَّهُ وَاجِبٌ.

وَلَا تَجُوْزُ طَاعَتُهُمَا فِي مَعْصِيَةِ اللهِ تَعَالَى، كَذَلِكَ نَصَّ عَلَيْهِ؛ لِقَوْلِ النَّبِيِّ ﷺ: «**لَا طَاعَةَ لِمَخْلُوْقٍ فِي مَعْصِيَةِ اللّٰهِ تَعَالَى**».

Sitting positions and gatherings

It is reprehensible to sit depending on one's left hand while it is behind one's back. Sitting between the sun and the shaded [areas] is likewise reprehensible.

Subsection

To conclude gatherings, it is recommended to say: 'Glory and all praise belongs to you Allāh! There is no god worthy of worship except you! I seek your forgiveness and repent to you!' This supplication will expiate any sins which may have occurred in the gatherings.

It is reprehensible to sit under the shades of minarets, to sweep the house using a piece of rag, and to drink from the broken parts of a vessel.

[Conclusion]

These things are a sum from manners and etiquettes, and what is correct is from Allāh the Exalted.

فَصْلٌ

وَيُكْرَهُ الاتِّكَاءُ عَلَى يُسْرى يَدَيْهِ وَرَاءِ ظَهْرِهِ. وَيُكْرَهُ الجُلُوْسُ بَيْنَ الشَّمْسِ وَالظِّلِّ.

فَصْلٌ

وَيُسْتَحَبُّ أَنْ يَقُوْلَ عِنْدَ النُّهُوْضِ مِنَ المَجْلِسِ: (سُبْحَانَكَ اللَّهُمَّ وَبِحَمْدِكَ، لَا إِلَهَ إِلَّا أَنْتَ، أَسْتَغْفِرُكَ وَأَتُوْبُ إِلَيْكَ) فَهِيَ كَفَّارَةُ المَجْلِسِ.

وَيُكْرَهُ الجُلُوسُ فِي ظِلِّ المَنَارَةِ، وَكَنْسُ البَيْتِ بِالخِرْقَةِ، وَالشُّرْبُ مِنْ ثُلْمَةِ الإِنَاءِ.

[الخاتمة]

فَهَذِهِ جُمْلَةٌ مِنَ الآدَابِ، وَاللّٰهُ تَعَالَى المُوَفِّقُ لِلصَّوَابِ.

Bibliography

[Arabic]

ʿAbdullāh Abū Zayd, Bakr. *Al-Madkhal Al-Mufaṣṣal*, 2 vols., Riyadh: Dār al-ʿĀsima, 1997.

Al-Fawzān, ʿAbdullāh. *Al-Fawāʾid al-majmūʿa fī sharḥ fuṣūl al-ādāb wa makārim al-akhlāq al-mashrūʿa,* Riyadh: Dār Ibn al-Jawzī, 2012.

Al-Ṭurīqī, ʿAbdullāh. *Al-Ḥanābila khilāl thalātha ʿashar qarnā,* 14 vols., Beirut: 2012.

Ibn al-Farrāʾ, Muḥmmad b. Muḥammad (Ibn Abī Yaʿlā). *Ṭabaqāt al-Ḥanābila,* 4 vols., Beirut: Dār al-Maʿrifa, 2004.

Ibn Mufliḥ, Muḥammad. *Al-Ādāb al-sharʿīya,* 4 vols., ed. Shuʾayb al-Arnāʾūṭ, Beirut: Muʾassasa al-Risāla, 2012.

[English]

Hatim, B. *Discourse and the Translator,* 1st Ed., New York: Longman Inc., 1990.

Ibn ʿAbd al-Hādī, Yusūf. *An Epitome of Ḥanbalī Substantive Law.* Translated by Jewel Jalil. Birmingham: Dar al-Arqam: 2018.

Makdisi, George. *Ibn ʿAqil: religion and culture in classical Islam,* Edinburgh: Edinburgh University Press, 1997.

Newmark, P. *A Textbook of Translation,* Hertfordshire: Prentice Hall International Ltd, 1998.

Nida, E. *Contexts in Translation,* Philadelphia: John Benjamins Publishing Co., 2001.